Life Balancing

An Easy Self Help Guide to Spiritual Development

Rachael Chitrakar

I would like to thank everyone whom I've had the pleasure of working with as this has enabled me to learn and develop the art of healing.

I would also like to say thank you to Paddy and Ann Vickers, who have edited and encouraged me to publish this book.

And my daughter Mischa Kerr who helped me design the cover and finishing touches!

Details for workshops and healing on website. Crystals can be bought from online shop.

www.naturalhealingshop.co.uk

Contents

Introduction

This book will help you learn how to achieve a contented and balanced life style which suits you. It is for those who are interested in developing their own spirituality and inner peace. In the process looking at all aspects of self and how to reach your full potential in life. The skills learnt will enable you to deal with the challenges of life.

It will empower you to move with confidence into whatever area of learning, interest or employment you wish to. Self-expression, self-worth and self-confidence, are essential prerequisites for stepping into who you are and what you want to achieve in life.

It is for people with a religious faith as well as those with a faith in spirituality but who do not adhere to a religion.

Life Balancing

The aim of this book is to give suggestions on how to work through personal issues which are affecting us in the present, in order to develop peace of mind, which in turn will have a positive physical benefit. Thus working towards balance and unity of mind, body and spirit. If we can achieve this on a personal level, we are helping in a step towards the unity of mankind. Communities consist of individuals, and how each person develops will affect the development of our society.

'So powerful is the light of unity that it can illuminate the whole earth.' 1 Baha'u'llah

We are all on a journey of self-discovery...

'True loss is for him whose days have been spent in utter ignorance of his self.' 2 Baha'u'llah

This is a journey of cleansing of self. It is not achieved overnight, but is a continual process, in which life will give opportunities for growth and consolidation of lessons learned.

As we become more aware of what is hidden in our subconscious and release what no longer serves us positively in our lives, we start the process of becoming more at peace within ourselves.

My Awakening to spirituality

My journey of self-awareness started with an illness, finding healing through working on the energies of the body with reflexology and Reiki, which in turn opened up the possibilities that there was more to me than my physical self.

I was beginning to be aware of my own energies and began learning how to do hands on healing. I started to see myself as a spiritual being with a physical body. I was full of doubt and rather scared of these new ideas. So when I began having dreams about spiritual concepts I dismissed them. The dreams changed to everyday things that came true. I dismissed these as well. One night I dreamt about someone having, what looked like, a heart attack. I was shown where to put my hands to give healing. The dream was so lucid with lots of detail. Two weeks later everything in my dream came true. I was shocked to say the least! I decided I could not dismiss my dreams any more. The dreams changed back to spiritual concepts. After many weeks of being woken up every night I finally found out what the dreams were trying to tell me about.....The Baha'i Faith!

Once I began looking into the Baha'i Faith the dreams gave me positive feedback that now I was on the right path. I was amazed to find that it was all about my beliefs on life and how we should live. The only difference was, I did not believe in God.
This caused me great problems at first. I did not want to be associated with a 'religion'! The friends I had been meeting were spiritual people, who were into spirituality without an organised faith. This in itself was enough of a jump for me....but a faith! The dreams had been so overwhelming that I could not dismiss where I was being led. So I studied the writings from the Baha'i Faith, read up all I could find on the subject. Finding books that were not written by Baha'is to see what others thought about it...was it a cult...etc.

Everything I read about the faith was positive and the writings revealed by Baha'u'llah, the founder of the faith, made so much sense to me.

I declared myself a Baha'i 4 weeks after finding out about the Faith. I just had an inner knowing that this was right for me, and I would have to work through my issues about God. This happened about 20 years ago and now I am in a very different place within myself.

There are many quotations in this book which are from the Baha'i Writings (these are in italics). There are also many from other sources. The rest of the book is my own opinion, taken from my own experience of life, and should not be taken as Baha'i teachings.

Some helpful attributes

There are qualities which enhance our lives, such as:

* Having a positive outlook

Stress is usually due to our attitudes to situations. To develop a positive outlook it helps to look at how we can learn from a given event. If negative emotions come up, it is best to look at why we feel as we do, this enables us to release these emotions and to step into greater faith and trust. We endeavour to step into a spiritual reality where we can see connections and significance of events, where we have a 'knowing' that everything is for our highest good and spiritual development. In all situations we can look at ourselves to see why a 'button' has been pushed. It is often due to unresolved issues within ourselves, which have been highlighted by others. Once the issue has been recognised and the internal cause resolved, no one can push that button again, because it has gone!

- A relaxed mind and body

This can be achieved through physical relaxation exercises, breathing exercises, visualisations/meditations, energy-balancing and prayer. Relaxing the mind and body refreshes the spirit.

- Self-confidence

To be able to express oneself with confidence physically, mentally, emotionally, creatively and spiritually; one has to let go of limiting fears, old thought patterns and behaviours, setting healthy personal boundaries, plus developing and using one's own intuition.

- Compassion and forgiveness

This needs to be developed for ourselves as well as applied to others. The more compassionate we are to our self the more compassion and forgiveness we will be able to have for others. Looking within will help develop these virtues.

- Detachment

This is not about ignoring a situation or pretending something does not matter. This is about working through thoughts and emotions that arise through an event until you have released the attachment to the issue. In this process one can step into greater faith and attachment to God.

- Faith

Faith is having complete trust in the process of life. 'Knowing' everything is for our highest good. Again, looking within helps this process.

- Inner peace

Inner peace is achieved when putting all of the above into action.

Plus, it is greatly enhanced with a knowledge of God, love of God, acceptance of the Will of God, service to mankind, and development of virtues.

These last concepts I personally have found through studying the writings of Baha'u'llah. It is an ongoing process which deepens as time passes by.

To develop these qualities, it is helpful to learn how to quieten the mind, and letting go of all the chatter of a busy mind. One can then discern the intuitive useful information that can be found in the peaceful mind.

This book has three sections: quietening of the mind, working on self, and developing the spirituality of your life.

Quietening the Mind

There are many ways to learn how to quieten the mind:

- **Relaxation**

Relaxation is healing in itself - releasing tension, relaxing mind and body, aiding concentration for meditation and visualisation.

At first it may seem hard - the mind will create many reasons for not practising. We are learning to be master of our mind and emotions and not allowing them to control us.

Try to practise every day.

I have found a simple and effective relaxation exercise.

Start by lying down with a pillow beneath your head. Cover yourself with a blanket to keep warm. Lie straight, rest arms about 6 inches away from body with palms upwards.

Watch your thoughts, and release them.

Let thoughts about home and work float away.

Focus on your physical body. Bring your attention to your:

Toes....tense them.....and relax them.

Feet.....tense them.....and relax them.

Release the tension so your feet feel heavy.

Calves/shins....tense them.....and relax them.

Knees/thighs....tense them.....and relax them.

Release the tension so your legs feel heavy.

Buttocks.....tense them.....and relax them.

Abdomen....tense the muscles that surround the pelvic girdle and also the organs that are contained inside. Be aware of the discomfort.....relax.

Solar plexus (this area is affected when we face fear - causing 'butterflies')

..... tense the muscles and organs such as stomach, pancreas and liver.

Note how you feel.....relax.

Chest.... mentally see inside and feel the gentle rhythm of your heart beating, release tension. Visualise your diaphragm stretching down into your abdomen as your lungs inflate and returning to its normal position when your lungs deflate during exhalation.

Release the tension.

Shoulders, arms and hands....tense them.....and relax them.

Release the tension.

Throat and neck, release tension.....relax and allow neck and shoulders to be heavy and at rest.

Head...screw up your face, eyes, jaw and tongue.....and relax, including your forehead and the back of your head. Feel as though your head is sinking into the ground.

Scan your body and check if there is any tension which needs releasing.

You can do this exercise sitting in a chair - then you are relaxed and ready for a visualization or meditation.

Breathing exercises are good for relaxation, oxygenating the body, and cleansing the air in the lungs. The following four breathing exercises I have found to be very helpful.

To ventilate and cleanse the lungs;

Inhale, retaining the air for a few seconds.

Pucker the lips, as if to whistle, (don't swell out cheeks), sharply exhale a little air.

Stop for a moment, holding the breath, then exhale a little more.

Repeat until air is completely exhaled.

Do not repeat the whole process for more than two inhalations.

This full breath exercise is good for cleansing and relaxation. Practise this exercise in three parts before you put it together as one movement.

1.Place hands lightly on your abdomen.
Think of a balloon to be filled and then totally emptied.
Exhale.
Slowly breathe in through your nose.
Feel hands spreading apart and separating.
Slowly exhale through nose. Feel hands contracting.
Empty completely.
Try 3 times, aiming for a bigger balloon each time.

2.Place hands on rib cage. Think of the ribs as an accordion.
Exhale.
Inhale slowly. Feel tissue expanding.
Exhale.

3.To operate the upper section of the lungs.
Exhale short puffs of air until empty.
Inhale short puffs of air until full.
Exhale.

The three parts should be performed all together as one movement on the 'in' breath. On the 'out' breath, lower the shoulders, contract the ribs and pull in the abdomen.

This rhythmic breathing exercise is calming:
Sit erect, chest, head and neck in a straight line, shoulders slightly back, and hands resting on lap.
Inhale slowly, counting to 6.

Retain breath and count to 6.
Exhale slowly through the nostrils, counting to 6.
Count to 6, holding between breaths.
Repeat this process a number of times, but avoid fatiguing yourself. If counting to 6 is too long, count with a number that feels comfortable.

A breathing exercise for clearing and balancing the brain. A good one to do when you wake up.
Sit upright.
Press left nostril closed with thumb and inhale through right nostril.
Remove thumb, close right nostril with forefinger and exhale through left nostril.
Without changing fingers, inhale through left nostril.
Change fingers, exhale through right.
Inhale through the right and exhale through the left, and so on...

One can enhance this process by placing first and second finger on your forehead (brow chakra) whilst using thumb and fourth finger to open and close the nostrils.

- **Meditation**

Meditations are designed to help you relax and free the mind of everyday thoughts. This can be achieved by concentrating the mind on an image, sound, movement or breathing. This skill puts you in touch with your inner thoughts and feelings, your intuitive knowledge.

'It is an axiomatic fact that while you meditate you are speaking with your own spirit. In that state of mind you put certain questions to your spirit and the spirit answers: the light breaks forth and the reality is revealed.' 3 Abdu'l-Baha

'The inspiration received through meditation is of a nature that one cannot measure or determine. God can inspire into our minds things that we had no previous knowledge of, if He desires to do so.' 4 written on behalf of Shoghi Effendi

Start with a few minutes a day and build upon this. Be patient with yourself. Do not expect to start seeing/knowing/obtaining insights as you may become stressed and disheartened! The process is the achievement not a 'desired' outcome. Accept the meditation exactly as it is. Everyone has to learn how to develop these skills and apply them. The first step is quietening the mind of 'chatter'. Then the insights will come to you in their own way - have no expectations of how. Find a meditation method that suits you. Below are a few exercises you can try - the breath meditation is good because you do not need any props, and can do it whenever convenient.

Meditation on the breath
Sit with spine straight and shoulders both down and back slightly.
Close eyes and relax.
Notice your breath flowing in and out.
Turn your attention to where your breath is going inside your body.
Breathe deeply into your abdomen.
Bring your concentration to your nostrils where the air enters and leaves the body.
Feel the cool air as you breathe in and the warm air as you breathe out.
Count each 'out' breath from one to ten, then start again.
If your attention wanders, go back to one.

Be patient; lapses of attention happen to everyone. To keep my mind focussed I had to count one for 'out' breath and one for 'in' breath etc.

With regular practice your concentration span will increase.

If you are able to do this for about 15 minutes, you may give up counting - your breath naturally becomes irregular.

This candle meditation I have found difficult, but some people find it easy.

Place a lighted candle about 3 foot away.

Concentrate on the flame without blinking.

Close your eyes.

In front of your closed eyes should appear the flame of the candle.

When the image disappears, try and bring it back into focus.

Repeat from beginning.

The objective is to hold the flame in focus with closed eyes, keeping the image for as long as possible.

Meditation on the feel of an object.

Choose an object (not sharp or heavy).

Sit and close your eyes.

Concentrate on the texture of the object.

Try and detach your mind from what the object is, focus your attention on how it feels.

Crystals are excellent to use in this way. Many people believe crystals have energies vibrating at various frequencies which affect us when held or placed on oneself. Collect a selection of crystals - they do not need to be large, expensive ones. You do not need knowledge about the effects of crystals. Use your intuition. In other words, choose one or two of your crystals that you feel like using, and hold it/them in your hands. Sit quietly and breathe deeply for a few minutes. Then bring your awareness to your body and notice if you feel any sensations or slight pains. It maybe that the energies of the crystals are affecting you and you are now trying to tune in to what is happening on an energy level. When energy is being balanced or moved you may feel this by differences in temperature, tingling sensations, slight pains, pulsing or suchlike. Notice any differences you feel in your body. Do you usually suffer with pain which feels different when holding the crystals? Try this meditation using different crystals and notice the effects. Whichever crystals you are drawn to will be helping you in some way. It is helpful to hold crystals during any meditations or breathing exercises; it increases the overall benefits. Most people find that crystals enhance their ability to quieten the mind and to relax.

Listening to music can be a very enjoyable way to meditate. Choose any music you feel like listening to. Calm music can be good for calming and relaxation. Loud rhythmic drumming may give energy, vitality, or release repressed emotions. Experiment and choose according to your needs.

Meditation using sound is good. Sound is a vibration which affects our energies. Tibetan singing bowls are used in this way. The different pitches affect us in different ways. Again, choose according to your need at the time.

One can use a mantra. Mantras are sounds which are repeated slowly and deeply so that they resonate. When we deliberately and consciously sound a mantra we are gradually changed by its dual aspects: meaning and vibration. As we internalise the concept represented by the mantra we absorb new ideas in consciousness. Sound is powerful.

Either of these phrases I have found to be good as a mantra:

Alláh-u-Abhá   meaning   God the All-Glorious.

Yá Bahá'u'l-Abhá   meaning   O Thou Glory of Glories!

Baha'is repeat the invocation Alláh-u-Abhá every day. The power of these words affects your whole being.

Baha'is also meditate on the words revealed by Baha'u'llah. Because (as Baha'i's believe) these are the words of God for this age, there is a great potency within them.

Mandalas can be used for meditation. The word mandala originates from Sanskrit and means centre, circumference or magic circle. The mandala consists of a circle and a centre point. The centre point symbolises unity, perfection, and the Divine part of us which is eternal. In some cultures it is the symbol of God. The circle is a symbol of eternity, a line which has no beginning or end.
Find a mandala which appeals to you and study it. Unless otherwise stated, work from the outer edge of the circle to the centre. The outer circle represents where we stand at this precise moment in time. It stands for our present understanding and appreciation of life. Keep your concentration on the mandala, bringing your mind back to the mandala if it wanders. Reflect upon what the symbols mean to you. There is a great deal to be learned by meditating in this way. I have found it very interesting meditating on mandalas that represented each chakra (energy centre). It is easy to Google for the required mandala.

- **Visualisation**

Visualisations are a powerful and effective tool. They can be used to relax the mind and body. Visualisation is a means of gathering energy. Our lives and circumstances are a projection or a product of our thoughts. Energy follows thought. The subconscious mind responds to thoughts, whether they are negative or positive. For visualisation to be effective, energy needs to be gathered to strengthen the mind in a creative way. Visualising nature automatically helps to regenerate the heart. Tensions and fear will be replaced by peace and calm. All the colours of nature touch the consciousness and affect the body by helping it to release blocked energy. Different symbols and colours move a person to different levels of awareness within themselves.

Visualisation is an active process, whereas meditation is a passive process.

The following visualisations I have found helpful. If you can visualise the scenes in your mind the pictures will tell you a lot about yourself and help you sort out inner issues. The scenes and symbols will be personal to you and interpret them with respect to what they represent for you. If your mind does not see in pictures go with your thoughts and emotions that the story evokes. However you interpret the stories try and keep your mind focussed on the visualisation, if it wanders, bring yourself back to the story. This does get easier with practice, and your inner guidance will develop.

Read the visualisation and remember it, then close your eyes and run through it in your mind. Or if easier record it and play it back to yourself.

Visualisation for Emotional Cleansing

Sit or lie down, make yourself comfy, close eyes.
Take some deep breaths and release tension from body.
Imagine yourself barefoot and standing on soft green grass on a hillside.
It is a beautiful warm, sunny day, the sky is blue.
There are trees and wild flowers.
You can see butterflies, birds and animals.
As you walk, feeling the soft green grass, inhale deeply, visualising light entering with each breath in, and on the outbreaths have the intention of releasing old thought patterns which are restricting your life.
You see a lake a short distance away.
Walk over to it.
The water is pure and has a silvery sheen.
You may swim in the water or sit by the lake and reflect.
If you choose to swim in this lake the water will gently remove negativity, cleansing your energies, changing darkness into light.
The negativity may be fears, lack of confidence, or feelings of low self-worth.
Release all negativity.
Some energies need letting go of.
Some energies need cleansing and keeping.
You will intuitively know which is which.
As you are swimming in the refreshing water, look to see if there are any emotional cords of energy attached to other people. These need to be gently released, with the intention of the energies being cleansed and given back to whom they belong.
The emotional attachments may be your own and need to be removed from others, cleansed and used to empower yourself.

Swim and enjoy the feelings of lightness and freedom from your own and other people's fears, demands and unrealistic expectations.
Feel the light entering your heart and spreading through to the whole of your being. You are light, bright and full of love, hope and joy!
When you have finished swimming, lie in the warm sun on the soft green grass.
The heat of the sun energises you.
You are ready for new beginnings!

Visualisation to Help One Move Forward in Life.

This next simple journey will reveal a great deal; all impressions will have symbolic overtones; try to interpret them after the visualisation.

Sit or lie down, make your body relaxed and comfy.
Close your eyes and create the following scenes in your imagination.
You are walking down a country lane.
You see a stile. Climb over it into a field dotted with wild flowers.
Listen to the sounds of insects and birds.
The field slopes gently down to a stream.
Walk across to the stream and sit by its bank.
Listen to the sound of running water.
The stream is narrow - find a way to cross it.
Explore this side of the stream. What can you see? What can you hear?
There is a building in the distance.
Stand in front of it.
Look carefully at what you can see.
Enter the building.
Pay attention to all that you see.

You will find a table.
On this table is a large book.
It has your name inscribed on the cover.
Stand before the book and compose your thoughts.
You have come to find a sign or symbol that will teach you something of significance about yourself.
Reflect on what you seek and why.
When you are ready open the book.
On the page you will find an image, a picture, a drawing or a shape.
Look carefully at what you see so you remember it.
When you are ready to leave, retrace your steps, out of the house, cross the stream, over the stile and back.

Healing Visualisation

The following visualisation is good for general healing. Try doing it regularly for a while. You will be working on a deeper level each time.

Sit down, clench muscles, and relax them.
Make your body relaxed and comfy.
Close your eyes and breathe into your abdomen.
Imagine a golden ball of light over your stomach.
The golden light is love and wisdom.
Breathe the light into your stomach.
Release tensions.
Breathe in the light and relax.
Stay with this for a while.
Imagine a second ball of golden light around your head.
Breathe it into your mind, fill your mind with the light of love and wisdom.
Worrying thoughts and anxieties drift away.
Your mind is transformed and becomes full of golden light.

Breathe in the light and relax.

Stay with this for a while.

Imagine a third ball of golden light over your heart.

Breathe it into your heart.

As you breathe allow yourself to smile, helping to open your heart to the light. Breathe in the light and relax.

Imagine your heart is a sparkling and gleaming crystal cave full of golden light.

In the cave a golden angel of healing welcomes you.

You are surrounded in a loving radiance.

You become aware of a stream of healing energy flowing towards you from the angel's heart.

Pause for a least two minutes.

Think of two or three words to describe how you feel.

Notice any changes in your body.

In your own time bring your awareness back to the room.

Remember to ground yourself.

An effective way to ground yourself is to imagine you are a tree.

The roots of your tree should be strong and travel deep down into the ground.

The tree above should be large and healthy.

The pictures that come to mind as you visualise your tree will represent your energies.

Think of the leaves absorbing water and it flowing down to the roots.

Then imagine the roots absorbing nutrients and these flowing up to the leaves.

Make the image as strong and healthy as possible.

When I first did this exercise, my tree roots just crept along the surface of the ground. I had to work regularly on this image to get strong healthy roots. I had to ask why I could not form roots and I found it was due to fears. As I worked on releasing these my root system became stronger.

When you ask yourself questions go with whatever pops into your head. It is often the little things you think "No can't be!" which on an unconscious level are affecting you. We have all collected weird and wonderful 'untruths' about ourselves!

- ➢ Acknowledge thoughts blocking the flow of energy.
- ➢ Change the negative thoughts into positive affirmations.
- ➢ The intention to release and change thoughts is the key to it happening.
- ➢ Thoughts that have been with you a long time may take a while to work through, over many sessions.
- ➢ Be patient and look for why you are retaining old thought patterns.
- ➢ It gets easier and quicker with practice.

A Cleansing Visualisation

And lastly a very short but effective visualisation to help removal of colds, flu and energy blockages.

Sit down and make your body relaxed and comfy.

Close your eyes and imagine sitting in front of a roaring log fire.

You are holding a large flat sieve.

The wires are very close together, making the holes minute.

Take the sieve and place it under your feet.

Imagine raising the sieve through your feet, your body to the top of your head.

As your body passes through the sieve, visualise catching any virus or unwanted bacteria in the sieve.
In order to destroy the virus or bacteria place the sieve into the fire.
You can use this concept with energy blocks.
Have the fire cleanse the energies which will be returned to you if needed.
Repeat this visualisation as many times as you feel necessary.

- **Prayer**

Prayer is an effective way of finding peace and quiet within. Apart from the power of the prayer it can be used like a meditation by keeping one's mind focussed on the prayer. Pray with the intention of finding peace and quiet. Try opening a prayer book with the intention of being given a prayer you need, or choose prayers you like.
If you have never particularly been into prayers, try it...it works!

If you have not got a prayer book I personally like the Baha'i prayers which are for all occasions and are acceptable to people from all different faiths.
One can find them on www.bahaiprayers.org

'Many find a difficulty in believing in the efficacy of prayer because they think that answers to prayer would involve arbitrary interference with the laws of nature. An analogy may help to remove this difficulty. If a magnet be held over some iron filings the latter will fly upwards and cling to it, but this involves no interference with the law of gravitation. The force of gravity continues to act on the filings just as before. What has happened is that a superior force has been brought into play—another force whose action is just as regular and calculable as that of gravity. The Bahá'í view is that prayer brings into action higher forces, as yet comparatively little known; but there seems no reason to believe that these forces are more arbitrary in their action than the physical forces. The difference is that they have not yet been fully studied and experimentally investigated, and their action appears mysterious and incalculable because of our ignorance. Another difficulty which some find perplexing is that prayer seems too feeble a force to produce the great results often claimed to it. Analogy may serve to clear up this difficulty also. A small force, when applied to the sluice gate of a reservoir, may release and regulate an enormous flow of water-power, or, when applied to the steering gear of an ocean liner, may control the course of the huge vessel. In the Bahá'í view, the power that brings about answers to prayer is the inexhaustible Power of God. The part of the suppliant is only to exert the feeble force necessary to release the flow or determine the course of the Divine Bounty, which is ever ready to serve those who have learned how to draw upon it.' 5 Dr JE Esslemont

I like these prayers;

Create in me a pure heart, O my God, and
renew a tranquil conscience within me, O my Hope!
Through the spirit of power confirm Thou me in Thy
Cause,
O my Best-Beloved, and by the light of Thy glory
reveal unto me Thy path, O Thou the Goal of my desire!
Through the power of Thy transcendent might lift me
up
unto the heaven of Thy holiness, O Source of my being,
and by the breezes of Thine eternity gladden me,
O Thou Who art my God!

Let Thine everlasting melodies breathe tranquillity on
me,
O my Companion, and let the riches of Thine ancient
countenance
deliver me from all except Thee, O my Master,
and let the tidings of the revelation of Thine
incorruptible
Essence bring me joy,
O Thou who art the most manifest of the manifest
and the most hidden of the hidden!

Baha'u'llah

This next prayer is wonderfully encouraging and uplifting, and comes from "Star of the West", which was an early Baha'i magazine:

O God! Refresh and gladden my spirit. Purify my heart.
Illumine my powers. I lay all my affairs in Thy hand.
Thou art my Guide and my Refuge.
I will no longer be sorrowful and grieved;
I will be a joyful and happy being.
O God! I will no longer be full of anxiety,
nor will I let trouble harass me.
I will not dwell on the unpleasant things of life.
O God! Thou art more friend to me than I am to myself.
I dedicate myself to thee, O Lord.

'Prayer and meditation are very important factors in deepening the spiritual life of the individual, but with them must go also action and example, as these are the tangible result of the former. Both are essential.' 6

Shoghi Effendi

- **Use positive thought as affirmations**

Choose your own thoughts or use positive thought cards. All thoughts need to be in the present tense. As though whatever is needed has already happened. You are stepping into owning this new belief system.

Look at your negative thoughts and change them into the positive. Repeat the positive many times a day, it helps in letting go of the old belief system, which you have probably repeated hundreds and thousands of times in various ways.

You can meditate upon the positive messages from angel cards.

An example of an affirmation which may be used after a healing visualisation:
I love my physical body, my thoughts and my feelings. This love I perceive as a pale pink mist which softly envelopes each cell of my body, creating health, peace and harmony.

Gratitude as an affirmation has positive effects......*'Be thou happy and well pleased and arise to offer thanks to God, in order that thanksgiving may conduce to the increase of bounty'.* 7 Abdu'l-Baha

- **Walking in the countryside or by the sea**

The body needs physical exercise to keep healthy. Walking in the countryside or by the sea has a very beneficial effect upon one's energies. As mentioned before, the colours are calming, and negative unwanted energies are released into the ground. I find the sea particularly good for cleansing one's energies.

Hugging trees with the intention of releasing blockages of energies is effective. Try using different species of tree and feel the effects.

You can use the walk as a moving meditation, using one's senses to see, smell, feel and hear. Keep your thoughts in the present. Also walking and reciting prayers is excellent.

Having learnt techniques to quieten the mind they can now be used. All of the skills covered so far will need to be practised regularly and used for working on the self. Be patient with oneself. Everyone has to learn how to develop these skills and apply them. Start with a few minutes a day and build upon this. Accept the visualising/meditation exactly as it is. With regular practice you will obtain results. Even with prayer we become more aware with time and practice…..

Intone, O My servant, the verses of God
that have been received by thee,
as intoned by them who have drawn
nigh unto Him,
that the sweetness of thy melody
may kindle thine own soul,
and attract the hearts of all men.
Whoso reciteth, in the privacy of his chamber,
the verses revealed by God,
the scattering angels of the Almighty
shall scatter abroad the fragrance
of the words uttered by his mouth,
and shall cause the heart
of every righteous man to throb.
Though he may, at first, remain unaware
of its effect, yet the virtue
of the grace vouchsafed unto him
must needs sooner or later exercise
its influence upon his soul.
Thus have the mysteries of the Revelation
of God been decreed
by virtue of the Will of Him
Who is the Source of power and wisdom. Baha'u'llah

Working on Self

What do we mean by self?

'Baha'u'llah explains [man's] personality, his consciousness, and his qualities remain in the degree of purity to which he attained in the physical realm. His progress in the next realm is infinite. The purpose of life in the physical world is to prepare the soul for its existence in the next. Just as an embryo develops its eyes, ears and limbs required for life outside the womb, so does an individual prepare in this world by developing spiritual qualities that provide him with the capacity for progress after death. The physical world is a world of hardship and suffering. It is by dealing with the difficulties that are an inherent part of material reality that the spiritual qualities are perfected.....

The material world..... is a learning environment for exploring spiritual reality. The material realm, being most accessible to human understanding, serves as a vehicle of metaphor and analogy to assist in comprehension of principles of spiritual reality. The understanding of these principles then finds expression through action in the physical realm: spiritual progress is dependent and conditioned on material means. It is ultimately by sacrificing the material characteristics of human nature that the individual is able to polish the mirror of the soul and manifest the true spiritual self.' [8]

Bahá'u'lláh's teachings explained by Paul Lample.

'*In the world of existence there is nothing so important as spirit, nothing so essential as the spirit of man. The*

25

spirit of man is the most noble of phenomena. The spirit of man is the meeting between man and God. The spirit of man is the animus of human life and the collective centre of all human virtues. The spirit of man is the cause of the illumination of this world.' 9

Abdu'l-Baha

The following are definitions of soul, spirit and mind taken from the Baha'i writings.

*'**Vegetable spirit** is the power of growth….*

***Animal spirit** is the power of all the senses….*

***Human spirit** ….rational soul…. as far as human ability permits, discovers the realities of things and becomes cognizant of their peculiarities and effects, and of the qualities and properties of beings….*

***Spirit of Faith**….comes from the breath of the Holy Spirit, and by the divine power it becomes the cause of eternal life….The human spirit, unless assisted by the spirit of faith, does not become acquainted with the divine secrets and heavenly realities. It is like a mirror which, although clear, polished and brilliant, is still in need of light. Until a ray of the sun reflects upon it, it cannot discover the heavenly secrets.*

***Mind** is the power of the human spirit. Spirit is the lamp and mind is the light which shines from the lamp. Spirit is the tree and mind is the fruit. Mind is the perfection of the spirit and is its essential quality, as the sun's rays are the essential necessity of the sun.*

***The Holy Spirit** is the bounty of God and the luminous rays which emanate from the Manifestations. It is the mediator between God and His creatures. It is like a mirror facing the sun. As the pure mirror receives light*

26

from the sun and transmits this bounty to others, so the Holy Spirit is the mediator of the Holy Light from the sun of reality, which it gives to the sanctified realities. It is adorned with all the divine perfections. Every time it appears, the world is renewed, and a new cycle is founded…. It can be compared to the spring; whenever it comes, the world passes from one condition to another…. Whenever it appears, it renews the world of humanity, and gives a new spirit to the human realities: it arrays the world of existence in a praiseworthy garment, dispels the darkness of ignorance, and causes the radiation of the light of perfections'….10 Abdu'l-Baha

'The journey of the soul from the beginning of its existence on earth is a process of growing in the understanding of the human spirit and the manifestation in action of its qualities. The journey involves hardship and struggle, and the desire to satisfy material needs often deflects a person from his true purpose. But perfecting the qualities of the spirit is the means for realizing the potentialities of one's true self, for achieving happiness and prosperity in this world and preparing the soul for its continuation in the next. At the moment of death, the soul departs from the body as a bird from a broken cage, and wings its way on an immortal journey through worlds of joy and unending progress.'11 Baha'u'llah's teachings

For centuries people have been aware of the energies (or chi) associated with the body. Using intuition people have described what they have felt or seen. I

27

have summarised below what are the most prevalent descriptions and thoughts about the energies. However, I do not personally sense them in this way. I see and feel the blocks in energies created by how we think. I can pick up the thoughts that are causing the blocks. I think these are veils between us and the light. Once they are removed the energy system becomes light and health is restored. Sometimes I see different colours of light and the meridians when working on them. I do not see the aura as a whole, but just where I need to help cleanse the energy system, and restore balance.

'God loves to attract a soul to Himself, but there are many barriers interposed between man and his Creator. These are all in the nature of attachment to material, intellectual and spiritual things which prevent man from drawing near to his God. These formidable barriers must be removed before man can draw near to God.' 12 Adib Taherzadeh

'Bahá'u'lláh states that there are three barriers between man and God. He exhorts the believers to pass beyond these so that they may attain His Presence. The first barrier is attachment to the things of this world, the second is attachment to the rewards of the next world, and the third is attachment to the Kingdom of Names.' 13 Adib Taherzadeh

Many complementary therapists believe there are seven main energy points, called chakras, which are positioned from the base of the spine up to the crown.

These large energy centres are linked with the body physically, mentally and emotionally. If they become out of balance this affects our health and wellbeing. Each chakra has a spiritual aspect relating to self, a dominant colour, and is linked to our endocrine glands and physical organs.

Crown Chakra

Spiritual self-awareness – recognising spiritual needs – love and respect for every part of self.

Centre of pure consciousness.

Associated with the pineal gland which regulates the onset of puberty, induces sleep and influences our moods.

Dominant colour violet.

Brow Chakra

Self-responsibility – taking responsibility of own life and needs.

Centre of visualisation and perception – reflects ego self/spiritual self, reasoning mind/intuitive mind, feminine/masculine.

Associated with the pituitary gland, eyes, nose, ears and brain.

Problems with this centre will include tiredness, irritability, confusion, rigid thoughts, sinus problems, catarrh, hay fever, sleeplessness, mental stress, neuritis and migraine.

Dominant colour indigo.

Throat Chakra

Self-expression – freedom to express oneself – creativity - centre of purification.

Associated with the thyroid and parathyroid, the nervous system, the vocal chords and the ears.

Dominant colour blue.

Heart Chakra

Self-love – appreciation of self – care of self – spiritual love for all.

Associated with the thymus, the heart and circulatory system, the lungs and respiratory system, the immune system and the arms and hands.

Dominant colours green and pink.

Solar Plexus Chakra

Self-worth – value own self and how this affects one's relationships.

Associated with the processes and organs of digestion and absorption, pancreas (islets of Langerhans), the breath, diaphragm, the stomach, duodenum, gall bladder and liver.

If this centre is unbalanced a person may have rapid mood swings, depression, introversion, lethargy, poor digestion and abnormal eating habits.

Dominant colour yellow.

Sacral Chakra

Self-respect – boundaries, with respect to self and others – emotions, fear and anxiety.

Associated with adrenal glands, flow of fluids in body, skin, female reproductive organs, the kidneys, bladder, circulatory system and lymphatic system.
If this centre is blocked women may not be able to reach orgasm and men may have premature ejaculation or the inability to achieve an erection.
Dominant colour orange.

Base Chakra
Self-awareness – awareness of own needs – physical energy and vitality – own will.
Associated with the gonads, legs, feet, bones, large intestine, spine and nervous system, regulates sense of smell.
If blocked may experience lack of energy. Sexual, fertility or menstrual problems.
Dominant colour red.

It is believed there are smaller energy points positioned over the body and all points large and small are connected via a network of energy channels called meridians. Many aspects of life affect our energies, for example: what we eat, the environment we live in, how we think, generally how we treat ourselves and others. Energy follows our thoughts, and most people have had many negative thoughts about themselves over the years. The negativity that builds up as a consequence affects the whole being.

'It is said that if you want to know what you were doing in the past, look at your body now; if you want to know what will happen to you in the future, look at what your mind is doing now.' 14 Dalai Lama

Everything about ourselves is reflected within our energies. Learning how to let go of old negative thought patterns, behaviours and fears will lead to a freeing up of the blocks. Negative and positive thoughts affect us on many levels.
We all communicate with each other on an energy level. It is easy to become linked into unhealthy energy situations. For example; some people make you feel drained and are drawing upon your energies, others we sympathise with too strongly and in trying to make them feel better we soak up their problem energies, we can be disempowered by giving energy to others, etc. One needs to learn how to be aware of our energy communications and balance ourselves so this does not occur. It is necessary to look at our past and present relationships, and it is very healthy for all concerned to give back to others what is theirs and retrieve what is yours.
Visualisations and positive affirmations work on an energy level and with regular practice you will become more aware of yourself. Learning to 'see' or 'feel' one's own energies is a very effective way of working on oneself. To begin with you are learning the methods of working on self, and with time the 'awareness' will gradually happen. Letting go of the need to see or feel in a certain way will allow your natural abilities to develop.

'If we are going to have some deeply spiritual experience we can rest assured God will vouchsafe it to us without having to look for it.' 15 written on behalf of Shoghi Effendi

'While admitting the reality of "supernormal" psychic faculties He deprecates attempts to force their development prematurely. These faculties will unfold naturally when the right time comes, if we only follow the path of spiritual progress which the Prophets have traced for us.' 16 Dr J.E. Esslemont summarising Abdu'l-Baha

'Briefly, there is no question that visions occasionally do come to individuals, which are true and have significance. On the other hand, this comes to an individual through the grace of God, and not through the exercise of any of the human faculties. It is not a thing which a person should try to develop. When a person endeavours to develop faculties so that they might enjoy visions, dreams etc., actually what they are doing is weakening certain of their spiritual capacities; and thus under such circumstances, dreams and visions have no reality, and ultimately lead to the destruction of the character of the person.' 17 written on behalf of Shoghi Effendi

The following is a visualisation on the chakras. It is a good way of perceiving the state of wellbeing your chakras are in, and then cleansing and strengthening them by brightening the dominant colour of each chakra. This is a powerful visualisation and you need to remember to ground yourself afterwards to make sure your energies are balanced after you have been working on them.

Sit with a straight back or stand.
Close your eyes and take a few deep breaths.
Release tensions from your mind and body.
Take your attention to your base chakra. (Base of spine).
Visualise the colour red.
Which shade of red do you see?
Using your imagination cleanse the red and make it the red of a red rose.
Focus on the red.
Move your attention up to your sacral chakra. (Just below the tummy button).
Visualise orange.
Which shade of orange do you see?
Using your imagination cleanse the orange and make it the orange colour like the fruit.
Focus on the colour orange.
Move your attention up to your solar plexus. (Just below your sternum).
Visualise yellow.
Which shade of yellow do you see?
Visualise a ball of yellow sun.
Focus on the yellow.
Move your attention up to your heart chakra
Visualise green and pink.
Which shades of green and pink do you see?
Visualise fresh green grass with wild pink flowers.
Focus on these colours.
Move your attention up to your throat chakra.

Visualise turquoise.
Which shade of turquoise do you see?
Imagine a clear bright turquoise.
Focus on turquoise.
Move your attention up to your brow chakra. (Mid forehead)
Visualise indigo.
Which shade of indigo do you see?
Imagine a deep, rich, dark blue.
Focus on indigo.
Move your attention to your crown chakra. (Top of head)
Visualise violet.
Which shade of violet do you see?
Imagine a dark amethyst crystal.
Focus on violet.

When you split white light with a prism you find the white light consists of many colours. This has bearing with respect to the energies/lights of the body.

'That divine world is manifestly a world of lights; therefore man has need of illumination here...' 8 Abdu'l-Baha

'Man is said to be the greatest representative of God, and he is the Book of Creation because all the mysteries of beings exist in him. If he comes under the shadow of the True Educator and is rightly trained, he becomes the essence of essences, the light of lights, the spirit of spirits; he becomes the centre of the divine appearances, the source of spiritual qualities, the

rising-place of heavenly lights, and the receptacle of divine inspirations. If he is deprived of this education he becomes the manifestation of satanic qualities, the sum of animal vices, and the source of all dark conditions.' [19] Abdu'l-Baha

The powers of prayers are incredible: I can personally 'see' and 'feel' them affecting our energies. I do not fully understand or see all of their effects, but I have no doubts that they work!
I have noticed that many people pray for others, but forget to pray for themselves. There are often issues around lack of self-worth that prevent praying for oneself. It is an essential part of one's development to pray for self and others in both this world and the next.

I think prayers help us cleanse ourselves energetically. For example sins are the veils between us and God, the veils that are of our making. On an energy level, blockages that prevent us from fully receiving the love of God. Veils which occur due to transgressions from the Baha'i teachings (if a Baha'i), and our negative thoughts which stem from how we feel about ourselves.

I also feel we can be affected by the energies from our ancestors and sometimes when cleansing our own present-day self we have to look back to our ancestral energies to release negative patterns from our lives, which are causing veils between ourselves and God.
'The unity of humanity as taught by Bahá'u'lláh refers not only to men still in the flesh, but to all human beings, whether embodied or disembodied. Not only all

36

men now living on the earth, but all in the spiritual world as well, are parts of one and the same organism and these two parts are intimately dependent, one on the other. Spiritual communion one with the other, far from being impossible or unnatural, is constant and inevitable. Those whose spiritual faculties are as yet undeveloped are unconscious of this vital connection, but as one's faculties develop, communications with those beyond the veil gradually become more conscious and definite. To the Prophets and saints this spiritual communion is as familiar and real as are ordinary vision and conversation to the rest of mankind.' 20 Dr J E Esslemont

Abdu'l-Baha explains about positive thoughts and prayers; how they affect mankind:
'If you desire with all your heart, friendship with every race on earth, your thought, spiritual and positive, will spread; it will become the desire of others, growing stronger and stronger, until reaches the minds of all men.' 21 Abdu'l-Baha

'Spirit has influence; prayer has spiritual effect. Therefore we pray…..'22 Abdu'l-Baha

The following are some prayers I have found effective. They are short enough to easily memorise and can be used as positive affirmations, mantras or invocations. Reciting them with whatever intention of need for that time. These prayers have a great potency because they were revealed by The Bab and Baha'u'llah, who are the latest Manifestations of God for this age.

Is there any remover of difficulties save God?
Say: Praised be God! He is God!
All are his servants, and all abide by His bidding!

The Bab

I bear witness, O my God, that Thou has created me to
know Thee and to worship Thee.
I testify, at this moment, to my powerlessness
and to Thy might, to my poverty and to Thy wealth.
There is none other God but Thee,
The Help in Peril, the Self-Subsisting.   Baha'u'llah

Learning to develop our intuition is a tool which is needed to help guide us through our life.

'He has given us material gifts and spiritual graces, outer sight to view the lights of the sun and inner vision by which we may perceive the glory of God. He has designed the outer ear to enjoy the melodies of sound and the inner hearing wherewith we may hear the voice of our creator.' 23 Abdu'l-Baha

Definition of intuition: Knowing something instinctively, the state of being aware of or knowing something without having to discover or perceive it, or the ability to do this.

Quietening the mind, meditation and prayer help you find your intuition. In the quiet you find the little voice that speaks to you with love. To develop your intuition you need to listen, trust and act upon it! You will learn to distinguish between Divine inspiration and imaginings or ego. Divine inspiration will always be for your highest good.

Healthy Choices

The only changes in life we can make are changes to our self. All the processes we have been looking at help you truly to look at yourself. The changes we make are towards bettering ourselves physically, mentally and spiritually.

We also have to look at our diet, environment and exercise. We all know what constitutes a healthy diet: fresh fruit, vegetables, plenty of water, etc... but it is putting it into practice. Balance is needed - no food should be forbidden, but adjust the quantity and frequency of foods you know are not very healthy for you. The more cleansed your body becomes the easier it is to be affected by foods and drinks. You may find there are certain foods or drinks you are better off avoiding altogether.

With respect to the environment we live in: clearing out cupboards and removing unused items and clutter from your living space will affect the flow of energies. Removal of clutter will enhance changes to take place within oneself. Also cleansing of oneself will lead to cleansing of one's surroundings.

Exercise helps to keep your body fit and healthy. On an energy level it helps one release blockages. Choose whichever type of exercise suits you. These following stretching exercises are helpful alongside your meditations and prayers.

Tall Stretch

Stand with feet about two inches apart.

Place hands by sides.

Straighten back, take back shoulders, open chest and extend neck.

Breathing in, stretch up arms over head until palms touch, arms as close to ears as possible.

Breathing out, bring arms back to sides.

Head Roll

Sitting, straighten spine, shoulders down and back, and chest open.

Exhaling, drop chin onto chest, feel stretch to back of neck.

Inhale, roll head around to right shoulder.

Exhale, continue to roll head backwards, feel stretch to throat.

Inhale, roll head round to left shoulder.

Exhale, roll head to front so chin rests on chest.

Continue this slow circular movement both clockwise and anticlockwise, whilst visualising all tension being released from neck.

Chest Expansion

Stand with feet about two inches apart.

Place hands by sides.

Straighten back, take back shoulders, open chest.

Keeping arms straight, clasp hands behind your back.

Keeping body upright, raise your arms behind you as far as possible.

This expands chest and releases tension from arms and shoulders.

With arms still raised, gently bend from waist as far as comfortable, hold for count of 5.

Raise body and gently bend backwards from waist, hold for count of 5.

Release, relax and repeat.

During exercise, visualise vertebrae as string of flower buds, each opening to show flowers of golden light - each petal radiating golden light via the nervous system from vertebrae to organs and muscles of the body.

Side Bend

Stand with feet about four inches apart.

Raise arms to shoulder level, palms facing down.

Keeping knees locked, slowly bend from waist to left side, attempt to touch left knee or thigh with left hand.

Repeat for right side.

Straighten and relax.

The Cat

Kneel on all fours, knees slightly apart, hands in line with knees and beneath shoulders.

Keeping arms straight, exhale whilst arching spine, contracting stomach muscles, moving chin towards chest bone.

Keeping arms straight, inhale whilst hollowing spine, so stomach drops towards floor, taking shoulders back and lifting head.

Continue movements slowly, visualising spine and separate movement of each vertebra becoming more and more supple.

To strengthen back and abdominal muscles
Sit on floor, legs in front, hands on thighs.
Slowly lower back to floor, raise arms over head, stretch whole body.
Bring hands to side, palms on floor.
Bend knees over abdomen then straighten.
Keeping legs straight, slowly lower to floor.
Place hands on thighs and slowly raise trunk back to sitting position.
Then slowly bend forward, sliding hands down to feet.
Return to sitting position and relax.

Developing Spirituality

The last section of this book is about developing the spirituality of our lives.

Using the dynamics of prayer for problem-solving is a skill which requires practice.

'It is not sufficient to pray diligently for guidance, but this prayer must be followed by meditation as to the best methods of action and then action itself. Even if the action should not immediately produce results, or perhaps not be entirely correct, that does not make so much difference, because prayer can only be answered through action and if someone's action is wrong, God can use that method of showing the pathway that is right.' 24 written on behalf of Shoghi Effendi

The five steps below were suggested by the Guardian of the Baha'i Faith. The steps are particularly helpful and clear to solving problems through prayer. When Shoghi Effendi mentions the Manifestations he is referring to Baha'u'llah and the Bab - the Founder and Forerunner of the Baha'i Faith.

'1st Step: Pray and meditate about it. Use the prayers of the Manifestations as they have the greatest power. Then remain in the silence of contemplation for a few minutes.
2nd Step: Arrive at a decision and hold this. This decision is usually born during the contemplation. It may seem almost impossible of accomplishment but if

it seems to be as answer to a prayer or a way of solving the problem, then immediately take the next step.

3rd Step: Have determination to carry the decision through. Many fail here. The decision, budding into determination, is blighted and instead becomes a wish or a vague longing. When determination is born, immediately take the next step.

4th Step: Have faith and confidence that the power will flow through you, the right way will appear, the door will open, the right thought, the right message, the right principle, or the right book will be given to you. Have confidence and the right thing will come to your need. Then, as you rise from prayer, take at once the 5th step.

5th Step: Act as though it had all been answered. Then act with tireless, ceaseless energy. And as you act, you, yourself, will become a magnet, which will attract more power to your being, until you become an unobstructed channel for the Divine power to flow through you. Many pray but do not remain for the last half of the first step. Some who meditate arrive at a decision, but fail to hold it. Few have the determination to carry the decision through, still fewer have the confidence that the right thing will come to their need. But how many remember to act as though it had all been answered? How true are these words "Greater than the prayer is the spirit in which it is uttered" and greater than the way it is uttered is the spirit in which it is carried out.' 25 Shoghi Effendi

The use of prayer is a very effective form of healing.

'*The most potent means of healing is the Power of the Holy Spirit.*

… This does not depend on contact, nor on sight, nor upon presence. … Whether the disease be light or severe, whether there be a contact of bodies or not, whether a personal connection be established between the sick person and the healer or not, this healing takes place through the power of the Holy Spirit.' 26 Abdu'l-Baha

'*The healing that is by the power of the Holy Spirit needs no special concentration or contact. It is through the wish or desire and the prayer of the holy person. The one who is sick may be in the East and the healer in the West, and they may not have been acquainted with each other, but as soon as that holy person turns his heart to God and begins to pray, the sick one is healed.*' 27 Abdu'l-Baha

'*There are two ways of healing diseases, the material way and the spiritual way. The first is the remedies of the physician; the second prayers and turning one's self to God. Both must be practised and followed. The diseases that happen to be caused by physical accident are cured by medical aid; others, which are due to spiritual causes, will disappear by spiritual means.*' 28 Abdu'l-Baha

'The power of spiritual healing is doubtless common to all mankind in greater or less degree, but, just as some men are endowed with exceptional talent for mathematics or music, so others appear to be endowed with exceptional aptitude for healing. These are the people who ought to make the healing art their lifework. Unfortunately, so materialistic has the world become in recent centuries that the very possibility of spiritual healing has to a large extent been lost sight of. Like all other talents the gift of healing has to be recognized, trained and educated in order that it may attain its highest development and power, and there are probably thousands in the world today, richly dowered with natural aptitude for healing, in whom this precious gift is lying dormant and inactive. When the potentialities of mental and spiritual treatment are more fully realized, the healing art will be transformed and ennobled and its efficacy immeasurably increased. And when this new knowledge and power in the healer are combined with lively faith and hope on the part of the patient, wonderful results may be looked for.' 29 Dr J.E. Esslemont

'This knowledge (of the healing art) is the most important of all the sciences, for it is the greatest means from God, the Life-giver to the dust, for preserving the bodies of all people, and He has put it in the forefront of all sciences and wisdoms. For this is the day when you must arise for My Victory.' 30 Baha'u'llah

'O handmaid of God! The power of the Holy Spirit healeth both physical and spiritual ailments' 31 Abdu'l-Baha

"Like all other talents the gift of healing has to be recognized, trained and educated in order that it may attain its highest development and power, and there are probably thousands in the world today, richly dowered with natural aptitude for healing, in whom this precious gift is lying dormant and inactive." [32] Dr J.E. Esslemont

I have taken this sentence from one of the quotes above because you may have this gift lying dormant and inactive!
To be an effective healer you need to work on yourself; cleansing your energies, to make yourself like a 'reed'.

'When the interior of a reed is empty and free from all matter, it will produce beautiful melodies; and as the sound and melodies do not come from the reed, but from the flute player who blows upon it, so the sanctified heart of that blessed Being is free and emptied from all save God, pure and exempt from the attachments of all human conditions, and is the companion of the Divine Spirit. Whatever He utters is not from Himself, but from the real flute player, and it is a divine inspiration.' [33] Abdu'l-Baha

'He who is filled with the love of Baha, and forgets all things, the Holy Spirit will be heard from his lips and the spirit of life will fill his heart….Words will issue from his lips in strands of pearls, and all sickness and disease will be healed by the laying on of hands.' [34] Abdu'l-Baha

Whilst giving healing I will recite prayers in my head or out loud if required. There is an added potency when reciting out loud. I think the sound energy of the words comes into effect. There is a short healing prayer which is easy to learn and recite. I find it very beneficial: I can see the energies unravelling and flowing when reciting it.

'The prayers which were revealed to ask for healing apply to both physical and spiritual healing. Recite them, then, to heal both the soul and the body.' 35

Abdu'l-Baha

Short Healing Prayer

Thy name is my healing, O my God, and remembrance of Thee is my remedy.
Nearness to Thee is my hope, and love for Thee is my companion.
Thy mercy to me is my healing and my succour in both this world and the world to come.
Thou, verily, art the All-Bountiful, the All-Knowing, the All-Wise.

Bahá'u'lláh

The Long Healing Prayer (below) is excellent. I read this and very deep healing takes place. The effects are wonderful. The following quote is by Shoghi Effendi about some of the prayers revealed by Baha'u'llah, the healing prayer is referring to this one.

'These daily obligatory prayers, together with a few other specific ones, such as the Healing Prayer, the Tablet of Ahmad, have been invested by Bahá'u'lláh with a special potency and significance, and should therefore be accepted as such and be recited by the believers with unquestioned faith and confidence, that through them they may enter into a much closer communion with God, and identify themselves more fully with His Laws and precepts.'36 letter written on behalf of Shoghi Effendi

The Long Healing Prayer

He is the Healer, the Sufficer, the Helper, the All-Forgiving, the All-Merciful.

I call on Thee O Exalted One, O Faithful One, O Glorious One!
Thou the Sufficing, Thou the Healing, Thou the Abiding, O Thou Abiding One!

I call on Thee O Sovereign, O Upraiser, O Judge! Thou the Sufficing,
Thou the Healing, Thou the Abiding, O Thou Abiding One!

I call on Thee O Peerless One, O Eternal One, O Single One!
Thou the Sufficing, Thou the Healing, Thou the Abiding, O Thou Abiding One!

I call on Thee O Most Praised One, O Holy One, O Helping One!
Thou the Sufficing, Thou the Healing, Thou the Abiding, O Thou Abiding One!

I call on Thee O Omniscient, O Most Wise, O Most Great One!

Thou the Sufficing, Thou the Healing, Thou the Abiding,
O Thou Abiding One!

I call on Thee O Clement One, O Majestic One, O
Ordaining One!
Thou the Sufficing, Thou the Healing, Thou the Abiding,
O Thou Abiding One!

I call on Thee O Beloved One, O Cherished One, O
Enraptured One!
Thou the Sufficing, Thou the Healing, Thou the Abiding,
O Thou Abiding One!

I call on Thee O Mightiest One, O Sustaining One, O
Potent One!
Thou the Sufficing, Thou the Healing, Thou the Abiding,
O Thou Abiding One!

I call on Thee O Ruling One, O Self-Subsisting, O All-
Knowing One!
Thou the Sufficing, Thou the Healing, Thou the Abiding,
O Thou Abiding One!

I call on Thee O Spirit, O Light, O Most Manifest One!
Thou the Sufficing,
Thou the Healing, Thou the Abiding, O Thou Abiding
One!

I call on Thee O Thou Frequented by all, O Thou Known
to all,
O Thou Hidden from all! Thou the Sufficing, Thou the
Healing,
Thou the Abiding, O Thou Abiding One!

I call on Thee O Concealed One, O Triumphant One, O Bestowing One!
Thou the Sufficing, Thou the Healing, Thou the Abiding, O Thou Abiding One!

I call on Thee O Almighty, O Succouring One, O Concealing One!
Thou the Sufficing, Thou the Healing, Thou the Abiding, O Thou Abiding One!

I call on Thee O Fashioner, O Satisfier, O Uprooter! Thou the Sufficing,
Thou the Healing, Thou the Abiding, O Thou Abiding One!

I call on Thee O Rising One, O Gathering One, O Exalting One!
Thou the Sufficing, Thou the Healing, Thou the Abiding, O Thou Abiding One!

I call on Thee O Perfecting One, O Unfettered One, O Bountiful One!
Thou the Sufficing, Thou the Healing, Thou the Abiding, O Thou Abiding One!

I call on Thee O Beneficent One, O Withholding One, O Creating One!
Thou the Sufficing, Thou the Healing, Thou the Abiding, O Thou Abiding One!

I call on Thee O Most Sublime One, O Beauteous One, O Bounteous One!

Thou the Sufficing, Thou the Healing, Thou the Abiding,
O Thou Abiding One!

I call on Thee O Just One, O Gracious One, O Generous
One!
Thou the Sufficing, Thou the Healing, Thou the Abiding,
O Thou Abiding One!

I call on Thee O All-Compelling, O Ever-Abiding, O Most
Knowing One!
Thou the Sufficing, Thou the Healing, Thou the Abiding,
O Thou Abiding One!

I call on Thee O Magnificent One, O Ancient of Days,
O Magnanimous One! Thou the Sufficing, Thou the
Healing,
Thou the Abiding, O Thou Abiding One!

I call on Thee O Well-guarded One, O Lord of Joy, O
Desired One!
Thou the Sufficing, Thou the Healing, Thou the Abiding,
O Thou Abiding One!

I call on Thee O Thou Kind to all, O Thou
Compassionate with all,
O Most Benevolent One! Thou the Sufficing, Thou the
Healing, Thou the Abiding, O Thou Abiding One!

I call on Thee O Haven for all, O Shelter to all, O All-
Preserving One!
Thou the Sufficing, Thou the Healing, Thou the Abiding,
O Thou Abiding One!

52

I call on Thee O Thou Succourer of all, O Thou Invoked by all,
O Quickening One! Thou the Sufficing, Thou the Healing,
Thou the Abiding, O Thou Abiding One!

I call on Thee O Unfolder, O Ravager, O Most Clement One!
Thou the Sufficing, Thou the Healing, Thou the Abiding,
O Thou Abiding One!

I call on Thee O Thou my Soul, O Thou my Beloved, O Thou my Faith!
Thou the Sufficing, Thou the Healing, Thou the Abiding,
O Thou Abiding One!

I call on Thee O Quencher of thirsts, O Transcendent Lord,
O Most Precious One! Thou the Sufficing, Thou the Healing, Thou the Abiding, O Thou Abiding One!

I call on Thee O Greatest Remembrance, O Noblest Name,
O Most Ancient Way! Thou the Sufficing, Thou the Healing, Thou the Abiding, O Thou Abiding One!

I call on Thee O Most Lauded, O Most Holy, O Sanctified One!
Thou the Sufficing, Thou the Healing, Thou the Abiding, O Thou Abiding One!

*I call on Thee O Unfastener, O Counsellor, O Deliverer!
Thou the Sufficing, Thou the Healing, Thou the Abiding,
O Thou Abiding One!*

*I call on Thee O Friend, O Physician, O Captivating
One! Thou the Sufficing, Thou the Healing, Thou the
Abiding, O Thou Abiding One!*

*I call on Thee O Glory, O Beauty, O Bountiful One!
Thou the Sufficing,
Thou the Healing, Thou the Abiding, O Thou Abiding
One!*

*I call on Thee O the Most Trusted, O the Best Lover, O
Lord of the Dawn!
Thou the Sufficing, Thou the Healing, Thou the Abiding,
O Thou Abiding One!*

*I call on Thee O Enkindler, O Brightener, O Bringer of
Delight!
Thou the Sufficing, Thou the Healing, Thou the Abiding,
O Thou Abiding One!*

*I call on Thee O Lord of Bounty, O Most Compassionate,
O Most Merciful One! Thou the Sufficing, Thou the
Healing, Thou the Abiding, O Thou Abiding One!*

*I call on Thee O Constant One, O Life-giving One, O
Source of all Being!
Thou the Sufficing, Thou the Healing, Thou the Abiding,
O Thou Abiding One!*

I call on Thee O Thou Who penetratest all things, O All-Seeing God,
O Lord of Utterance! Thou the Sufficing, Thou the Healing, Thou the Abiding, O Thou Abiding One!

I call on Thee O Manifest yet Hidden, O Unseen yet Renowned,
O Onlooker sought by all! Thou the Sufficing, Thou the Healing,
Thou the Abiding, O Thou Abiding One!

I call on Thee O Thou Who slayest the Lovers, O God of Grace to the wicked!
O Sufficer, I call on Thee, O Sufficer!
O Healer, I call on Thee, O Healer!
O Abider, I call on Thee, O Abider!
Thou the Ever-Abiding, O Thou Abiding One!
Sanctified art Thou, O my God! I beseech Thee by Thy generosity, whereby the portals of Thy bounty and grace were opened wide, whereby the Temple of Thy Holiness was established upon the throne of eternity; and by Thy mercy whereby Thou didst invite all created things unto the table of Thy bounties and bestowals; and by Thy grace whereby Thou didst respond, in thine own Self with Thy word "Yea!" on behalf of all in heaven and earth, at the hour when Thy sovereignty and Thy grandeur stood revealed, at the dawn-time when the might of Thy dominion was made manifest. And again do I beseech Thee, by these most beauteous names, by these most noble and sublime attributes, and by Thy most Exalted Remembrance, and by Thy pure and spotless Beauty, and by Thy hidden Light in

the most hidden pavilion, and by Thy Name, cloaked with the garment of affliction every morn and eve, to protect the bearer of this blessed Tablet, and whoso reciteth it, and whoso cometh upon it, and whoso passeth around the house wherein it is. Heal Thou, then, by it every sick, diseased and poor one, from every tribulation and distress, from every loathsome affliction and sorrow, and guide Thou by it whosoever desireth to enter upon the paths of Thy guidance, and the ways of Thy forgiveness and grace.

Thou art verily the Powerful, the All-Sufficing, the Healing, the Protector, the Giving, the Compassionate, the All-Generous, the All-Merciful.

Bahá'u'lláh

'*There is spiritual healing and there is also material healing. Unless these two work together a cure is impossible. The material element is medicine; spiritual healing is of God.*' 37 Abdu'l-Baha

We need to also remember that prayer and healing can help our loved ones who have departed from this physical world. The next quotes from Abdu'l-Baha (taken from Baha'u'llah and the New Era by Dr J E Esselmont P193), give explanations of why this is so.

Abdu'l-Bahá said to Miss E. J. Rosenberg in 1904: "*The grace of effective intercession is one of the perfections belonging to advanced souls, as well as to the Manifestation of God. Jesus Christ had the power of interceding for the forgiveness of His enemies when on earth, and He certainly has this power now. Abdu'l-Bahá never mentions the name of a dead person* without saying 'May God forgive him!' or words to that effect. Followers of the prophets have also this power of praying for the forgiveness of souls. Therefore we may not think that any souls are condemned to a stationary condition of suffering or loss arising from absolute ignorance of God. The power of effective intercession for them always exists." ...38 Abdu'l-Baha

"The rich in the other world can help the poor, as the rich can help the poor here. In every world all are the creatures of God. They are always dependent on Him. They are not independent and can never be so. While they are needful of God, the more they supplicate, the richer they become. What is their merchandise, their wealth? In the other world what is help and assistance? It is intercession. Undeveloped souls must gain progress at first through the supplications of the spiritually rich; afterwards they can progress through their own supplications."

Again He says: -- "Those who have ascended have different attributes from those who are still on earth, yet there is no real separation. In prayer there is a mingling of station, a mingling of condition. Pray for them as they pray for you!" - 'Abdu'l-Bahá in London.

39 Abdu'l-Baha

Asked whether it was possible through faith and love to bring the New Revelation to the knowledge of those who have departed from this life without hearing of it, 'Abdu'l-Bahá replied: -- "Yes, surely! Since sincere prayer always has its effect, and it has a great influence in the other world. We are never cut off from *those who are there. The real and genuine influence is not in this world but in that other."* - Notes of Mary Hanford Ford: Paris, 1911. 40 Abdu'l-Baha

Faith is an essential quality to foster. A definition of faith is: trust, strong belief, and unquestioning confidence. We need faith to become acquainted with the divine secrets and heavenly realities. The spirit of faith is bestowed upon us from the breath of the Holy Spirit, our faith is deepened by prayer and life experiences.

'*The essential purpose of faith and belief is to ennoble the inner being of man with the outpourings of grace from on high.'* 41 Abdu'l-Baha

'*Rid thou thyself of all attachments to aught except God, enrich thyself in God by dispensing with all else besides Him, and recite this prayer:*
Say: God sufficeth all things above all things, and nothing in the heavens or in the earth or in whatever lieth between them but God, thy Lord, sufficeth. Verily, He is in Himself the Knower, the Sustainer, the Omnipotent.
Regard not the all-sufficing power of God as an idle fancy. It is that genuine faith which thou cherishest for the Manifestation of God in every Dispensation. It is such faith which sufficeth above all the things that exist on the earth, whereas no created thing on earth besides faith would suffice thee. If thou art not a believer, the Tree of divine Truth would condemn thee to extinction. If thou art a believer, thy faith shall be

sufficient for thee above all things that exist on earth, even though thou possess nothing.' 42 The Bab

'Now this is the difference between one with faith and one without. A man of faith bears every trial, every hardship, with self-control and patience. One without faith is always wailing, lamenting, carrying on. He cannot endure hardship, he never thinks of better times coming that will take the place of present ills.' 43
Abdu'l-Baha

'And now I give you a commandment
which shall be for a covenant
between you and Me –
that ye have faith;

that your faith be steadfast as a rock
that no storms can move, that nothing can disturb,
and that it endure through all things
even to the end…….

As ye have faith
so shall your powers
and blessings be.
This is the balance –
this is the balance –
this is the balance.' 44 Abdu'l-Baha

'……Our afflictions, tests and trials are sometimes blessings in disguise, as they teach us to have more faith and confidence in God, and bring us nearer to Him' 45 written on behalf of Shoghi Effendi

'The essence of faith is fewness of words and abundance of deeds...' 46 Baha'u'llah

'Whatever hath befallen you, hath been for the sake of God. This is the truth, and in this there is no doubt. You should, therefore, leave all your affairs in His Hands, place your trust in Him, and rely upon Him. He will assuredly not forsake you. In this, likewise, there is no doubt. No father will surrender his sons to devouring beasts; no shepherd will leave his flock to ravening wolves. He will most certainly do his utmost to protect his own. If, however, for a few days, in compliance with God's all-encompassing wisdom, outward affairs should run their course contrary to one's cherished desire, this is of no consequence and should not matter. Our intent is that all the friends should fix their gaze on the Supreme Horizon, and cling to that which hath been revealed in the Tablets.' 47 Baha'u'llah

'In God, Who is the Lord of all created things, have I placed My whole trust. There is no God but Him, the Peerless, the Most Exalted. Unto Him have I resigned Myself and into His hands have I committed all My affairs.' 48 The Bab

'He does not ask us to follow Him blindly..... God has endowed man with a mind to operate as a torchlight and guide him to the truth. Read His words, consider His Teachings and measure their value in the light of contemporary problems and the truth will surely be revealed to you..... and you will appreciate the truth of

His Mission, as well as the true spirit He creates in whosoever follows His ways.' 49 written on behalf of Shoghi Effendi

Detachment is a virtue we acquire by examining ourselves. It may be helpful to detach from all sorts of aspects of life, such as others' opinions, status, behaviours..etc.

'Detachment does not consist in setting fire to one's house, or becoming bankrupt or throwing one's fortune out of the window, or even giving away all of one's possessions. Detachment consists in refraining from letting our possessions possess us. A prosperous merchant who is not absorbed in his business knows severance. A banker whose occupation does not prevent him from serving humanity is severed. A poor man can be attached to a small thing.' 50 Abdu'l-Baha

'We can appreciate without attaching ourselves to the things of this world. It sometimes happens that if a man loses his fortune he is so disheartened that he dies or becomes insane. While enjoying the things of this world we must remember that one day we shall have to do without them.' 51 Abdu'l-Baha

'Man must attach himself to an infinite reality, so that his glory, his joy, and his progress may be infinite. Only the spirit is real; everything else is as shadow. All bodies are disintegrated in the end; only reality subsists. All physical perfections come to an end; but the divine virtues are infinite.' 52 Abdu'l-Baha

'Well is it with him who hath been illumined with the light of trust and detachment. The tribulations of that Day will not hinder or alarm him.' 53 Baha'u'llah

'The world is but a show, vain and empty, a mere nothing, bearing the semblance of reality. Set not your affections upon it. Break not the bond that uniteth you with your Creator, and be not of those that have erred and strayed from His ways. Verily I say, the world is like the vapour in a desert, which the thirsty dreameth to be water and striveth after it with all his might, until when he cometh unto it, he findeth it to be mere illusion.' 54 Baha'u'llah

'O MY SERVANT!
Free thyself from the fetters of this world, and loose thy soul from the prison of self. Seize thy chance, for it will come to thee no more.' 55 Baha'u'llah

'Such is this mortal abode: a storehouse of afflictions and suffering. It is negligence that binds man to it for no comfort can be secured by any soul in this world, from monarch down to the least subject. If once it should offer man a sweet cup, a hundred bitter ones will follow it and such is the condition of this world. The wise man therefore does not attach himself to this mortal life and does not depend upon it; even at some moments he eagerly wishes death that he may thereby be freed from these sorrows and afflictions.' 56 Abdu'l-Baha

'The essence of detachment is for man to turn his face towards the courts of the Lord, to enter His Presence, *behold His Countenance, and stand as witness before Him.'* 57 Baha'u'llah

'The mind and spirit of man advance when he is tried by suffering. The more the ground is ploughed the better the seed will grow, the better the harvest will be. Just as the plough furrows the earth deeply, purifying it of weeds and thistles, so suffering and tribulation free man from the petty affairs of this worldly life until he arrives at a state of complete detachment. His attitude in this world will be that of divine happiness. Man is, so to speak, unripe: the heat of the fire of suffering will mature him. Look back to the times past and you will find that the greatest men have suffered most.' 58
Abdu'l-Baha

Inner peace is multifaceted, I feel this is achieved on a deep level by knowing we are spiritual beings in a physical body and developing our relationship with God.

'God in His Essence and in His Own Self hath ever been unseen, inaccessible, and unknowable.' 59 Baha'u'llah

'Knowledge is one of the greatest benefits of God. To acquire knowledge is incumbent upon all.' 60 Baha'u'llah

'...that which is the cause of everlasting life, eternal honour, universal enlightenment, real salvation and prosperity is, first of all, the knowledge of God. It is known that the knowledge of God is beyond all knowledge, and it is the greatest glory of the human world. For in the existing knowledge of the reality of

things there is material advantage, and through it outward civilization progresses; but the knowledge of God is the cause of spiritual progress and attraction, and through it the perception of truth, the exaltation of humanity, divine civilization, rightness of morals and illumination are obtained.' 61 Abdu'l-Baha

'The source of all learning is the knowledge of God, exalted be His Glory, and this cannot be attained save through the knowledge of His Divine Manifestation.' 62
Baha'u'llah

Baha'is believe the Divine Manifestation for this day is Baha'u'llah, who has revealed the words of God, giving social codes of conduct for unity through diversity. Baha'is believe in progressive revelation; which is, the prophets or manifestations of God, who founded all the main faiths, have given spiritual teachings to help our spiritual development and understanding. The essence of all the faiths is the same but the social teachings change according to man's capacity. We are all working towards …
'The earth is but one country, and mankind its citizens.'
63 Baha'u'llah

'The gift of God to this enlightened age is the knowledge of the oneness of mankind and of the fundamental oneness of religion. War shall cease between nations, and by the will of God the Most Great Peace shall come; the world will be seen as a new world, and all men will live as brothers.' 64 Abdu'l-Baha

Love is the greatest power, which we do not fully comprehend.

'... the love of God, the light of which shines in the lamp of the hearts of those who know God; its brilliant rays illuminate the horizon and give to man the life of the Kingdom. In truth, the fruit of human existence is the love of God, for this love is the spirit of life, and the eternal bounty. If the love of God did not exist, the contingent world would be in darkness; if the love of God did not exist, the hearts of men would be dead, and deprived of the sensations of existence; if the love of God did not exist, spiritual union would be lost; if the love of God did not exist, the light of unity would not illuminate humanity; if the love of God did not exist, the East and West, like two lovers, would not embrace each other; if the love of God did not exist, division and disunion would not be changed into fraternity; if the love of God did not exist, indifference would not end in affection; if the love of God did not exist, the stranger would not become the friend. The love of the human world has shone forth from the love of God and has appeared by the bounty and grace of God.' 65

Abdu'l-Baha

'There are four kinds of love. The first is the love that flows from God to man; it consists of the inexhaustible graces, the Divine effulgence and heavenly illumination. Through this love the world of being receives life. Through this love man is endowed with physical existence, until, through the breath of the Holy Spirit - this same love - he receives eternal life and becomes

65

the image of the Living God. This love is the origin of all the love in the world of creation.

The second is the love that flows from man to God. This is faith, attraction to the Divine, enkindlement, progress, entrance into the Kingdom of God, receiving the Bounties of God, illumination with the lights of the Kingdom. This love is the origin of all philanthropy; this love causes the hearts of men to reflect the rays of the Sun of Reality.

The third is the love of God towards the Self or Identity of God. This is the transfiguration of His Beauty, the reflection of Himself in the mirror of His Creation. This is the reality of love, the Ancient Love, the Eternal Love. Through one ray of this Love all other love exists.

The fourth is the love of man for man. The love which exists between the hearts of believers is prompted by the ideal of the unity of spirits. This love is attained through the knowledge of God, so that men see the Divine Love reflected in the heart. Each sees in the other the Beauty of God reflected in the soul, and finding this point of similarity, they are attracted to one another in love. This love will make all men the waves of one sea, this love will make them all the stars of one heaven and the fruits of one tree. This love will bring the realization of true accord, the foundation of real unity.' 66 Abdu'l-Baha

'Real love is the love which exists between God and His servants, the love which binds together holy souls. This is the love of the spiritual world, not the love of physical bodies and organisms.' 67 Abdu'l-Baha

'O Son of Being!
Love Me, that I may love thee.
If thou lovest me not,
My love can in no wise reach thee.
Know this O servant.'[68]

Baha'u'llah

Through prayer, meditation and actions one endeavours to adjust one's will to the Divine Will.

'If it be Thy pleasure, make me to grow as a tender herb in the meadows of Thy grace, that the gentle winds of Thy will may stir me up and bend me into conformity with Thy pleasure, in such wise that my movement and my stillness may be wholly directed by Thee.' [69] Baha'u'llah

'O thou who art turning thy face towards God! Close thine eyes to all things else, and open them to the realm of the All-Glorious. Ask whatsoever thou wishest of Him alone; seek whatsoever thou seekest from Him alone. With a look He granteth a hundred thousand hopes, with a glance He healeth a hundred thousand incurable ills, with a nod He layeth balm on every wound, with a glimpse He freeth the hearts from the shackles of grief. He doeth as He doeth, and what recourse have we? He carrieth out His Will, He ordaineth what He pleaseth. Then better for thee to bow down thy head in submission, and put thy trust in the All-Merciful Lord.' [70] Abdu'l-Baha

'Whatever God hath willed hath been, and that which He hath not willed shall not be. There is no power nor

strength except in God, the Most Exalted, the Most Mighty.' 71 The Bab

'Upon the tree of effulgent glory I have hung for thee the choicest fruits, wherefore hast thou turned away and contented thyself with that which is less good?' 72 Bahá'u'lláh

Service to mankind gives self-worth and satisfaction.

'Service to humanity is service to God...' 73 Abdu'l-Baha

'Is there any deed in the world that would be nobler than service to the common good? Is there any greater blessing conceivable for a man, than that he should become the cause of the education, the development, the prosperity and honour of his fellow-creatures? No, by the Lord God! The highest righteousness of all is for blessed souls to take hold of the hands of the helpless and deliver them out of their ignorance and abasement and poverty, and with pure motives, and only for the sake of God, to arise and energetically devote themselves to the service of the masses, forgetting their own worldly advantage and working only to serve the general good.' 74 Abdu'l-Baha

'In the Baha'i Cause arts, sciences and all crafts are (counted as) worship. The man who makes a piece of notepaper to the best of his ability, conscientiously, concentrating all his forces on perfecting it, is giving praise to God. Briefly, all effort and exertion put forth by man from the fullness of his heart is worship, if it is prompted by the highest motives and the will to do service to humanity. This is worship: to serve mankind and to minister to the needs of the people. Service is prayer. A physician ministering to the sick, gently, tenderly, free from prejudice and believing in the solidarity of the human race, he is giving praise.' [75]

Abdu'l-Baha

'The life of man is intended to be a life of spiritual enjoyment ...... This enjoyment depends upon the acquisition of heavenly virtues. The sublimity of man is his attainment of the knowledge of God. The bliss of man is the acquiring of heavenly bestowals, which descend upon him in the outflow of the bounty of God. The happiness of man is in the fragrance of the love of God. This is the highest pinnacle of attainment in the human world.' [76] Abdu'l-Baha

'In the beginning of his human life man was embryonic in the world of the matrix. There he received capacity and endowment for the reality of human existence. The forces and powers necessary for this world were bestowed upon him in that limited condition. In this world he needed eyes; he received them potentially in the other. He needed ears; he obtained them there in readiness and preparation for his new existence. The powers requisite in this world were conferred upon him in the world of the matrix, so that when he entered this realm of real existence he not only possessed all necessary functions and powers but found provision for his material sustenance awaiting him.

Therefore in this world he must prepare himself for the life beyond. That which he needs in the world of the Kingdom must be obtained here. Just as he prepared himself in the world of the matrix by acquiring forces necessary in this sphere of existence, so likewise the indispensable forces of the divine existence must be potentially attained in this world.

What is he in need of in the Kingdom which transcends the life and limitation of this mortal sphere? That world beyond is a world of sanctity and radiance; therefore it is necessary that in this world he should acquire these divine attributes. In that world there is need of spirituality, faith, assurance, the knowledge and love of God. These he must attain in this world so that after his ascension from the earthly to the heavenly Kingdom he shall find all that is needful in that life eternal ready for him.

That divine world is manifestly a world of lights; therefore man has need of illumination here. That is a world of love; the love of God is essential. It is a world of perfections; virtues or perfections must be acquired. That world is vivified by the breaths of the Holy Spirit; in this world we must seek them. That is the Kingdom of life everlasting; it must be attained during this vanishing existence.

By what means can man acquire these things? How shall he obtain these merciful gifts and powers? First, through the knowledge of God. Second, through the love of God. Third, through faith. Fourth, through *philanthropic deeds. Fifth, through self-sacrifice. Sixth, through severance from this world. Seventh, through sanctity and holiness. Unless he acquires these forces and attains to these requirements he will surely be deprived of the life that is eternal. But if he possesses the knowledge of God, becomes ignited through the fire of the love of God, witnesses the great and mighty signs of the Kingdom, becomes the cause of love among mankind, and lives in the utmost state of sanctity and holiness, he shall surely attain to second birth, be baptized by the Holy Spirit and enjoy everlasting existence.'* 77 Abdu'l-Baha

There are so many virtues which we can work on, think about and acquire. Here are some but I'm sure there are others...

Cleanliness	Good Language	Respect For
Compassion	Gratitude	Others
Concern	Happiness	Righteousness
Contentment	Honesty	Sacrifice
Co-operation	Hospitality	Self-Knowledge
Courage	Humility	Self-Respect
Courtesy	Joy	Service
Detachment	Justice	Sharing
Distinction	Kindness	Silence
Education	Knowledge	Sincerity
Faith	Liberty	Thoughts
Forbearance	Love	Tranquillity
Forgiveness	Obedience	Trust In God
Friendliness	Patience	Trustworthiness
Generosity	Peacefulness	Truthfulness
Giving	Prayer/Work as	Unity
Good Conduct	Prayer	Wisdom
	Purity	

Finally I find that if I reflect upon this simple first Hidden Word, I have to reflect on many virtues to keep my heart pure, kindly and radiant!

'O Son of Spirit!
My first counsel is this:
Possess a pure, kindly and radiant heart,
that thine may be a sovereignty ancient, imperishable
and everlasting.' [78]

Baha'u'llah

Appendix

This book is written using writings from the Baha'i Faith. There are many good books written about the Faith and there is the website www.bahai.org if you are interested to know more.

Baha'is believe in progressive revelation: meaning all the Manifestations of God, such as Abraham, Moses, Krishna, Zoroaster, Buddha, Jesus, Muhammad, the Bab and Baha'u'llah, have given the same essential spiritual message, but the social teachings are relevant for the age they are revealed in. Baha'is believe there will be other educators of men in the future, the next one being in approximately 1000 years.

Baha'u'llah is the Manifestation of God for whom all the faiths have been waiting. His teachings are about the oneness of mankind and the oneness of God. Baha'u'llah has revealed how to bring unity to this world from a spiritual perspective and a physical plan of how man can achieve this. There is only the one religion of God which has altered over time to educate man throughout his development on earth. Man is coming into the age of maturity and now every individual is responsible for his own development and relationship with God. In the past priests were needed to read and interpret the word of God. Now with education for all becoming a reality, people can read the latest words of God revealed by Baha'u'llah and put them into practice in their own lives. The transformative power of these words is immeasurable.

We are all aware that there are so many problems in the world today, Baha'u'llah has revealed answers of how to solve all of the issues, if we look to spiritually based solutions that can be applied to this physical reality in practical ways.

A Brief History of the Baha'i Faith

The Bab was born in 1819 in Shiraz, Iran. He was a Manifestation of God whose followers were called Babis. Thousands of people became His followers and many were gruesomely martyred. The Bab proclaimed a radical faith which foretold the coming of Baha'u'llah. In 1850, the new Shah and his prime minister decided the only way to stop this faith was to execute the Founder. The Bab was taken to Tabriz and tied up in a market place. A regiment of soldiers fired, but all of the shots missed and the Bab had disappeared. He was found dictating His last words to His secretary. He declared He was now ready, and was brought back to the market place. A new regiment of men was found, and this time He was killed. His body was rescued by some of His followers and hidden for over 50 years in various places, until finally it was laid to rest on Mount Carmel, in Haifa, Israel. Here a beautiful shrine has been erected, surrounded by wonderful gardens.

Baha'u'llah was born in Tehran, Iran, in 1817. He became a follower of the Bab and was for this reason, imprisoned in an underground pit, beaten and had heavy chains placed round His neck. It was here that Baha'u'llah had a visionary experience and became aware of His Station as a Manifestation of God. Baha'u'llah's life was spared due to His high social status, but He was exiled. He was exiled with His family to Iraq, then Turkey and finally to Akka in Israel.

In 1863, when in Baghdad, in Iraq, Baha'u'llah announced He was the Promised One of all the religions, whom the Bab had spoken about.

In Akka He was imprisoned at first within the citadel. Later, when this building was needed, He was placed under house arrest within the city. Over time His character became known and in 1879 He was allowed to live in the mansion of Bahji just outside of Akka.

During Baha'u'llah's life time He had to deal with so many difficulties, from losing His house, possessions and all human rights, to being imprisoned and subjected to unjust legal procedures. During exile His family suffered from poverty, hunger, and exposure, whilst in prison unhygienic conditions and overcrowding. Baha'u'llah and His wife had seen their children suffer illness and death due to the dreadful conditions.

Baha'u'llah spent the last years of His life writing, dictating many works, receiving pilgrims and directing the affairs of His religion. Unity is the key to the Baha'i Faith, and Baha'u'llah has put in place safeguards which will keep the faith united and upstanding, with respect to the individual Baha'is and the administrative bodies.

Baha'u'llah passed away on 29 May 1892. He was seventy-four years old, having spent 40 of those years as a prisoner and in exile. He is buried in a house next to the mansion of Bahji. Baha'is believe this to be the holiest place on earth. He appointed His eldest son, Abdul Baha, to lead the Baha'i community and to be the sole interpreter of his writings.

Abdul Baha was born in Tehran on 23 May 1844. Living His life through His father's teachings, He too lived a life of exile and imprisonment with His father and family. But eventually He was allowed His freedom and at the age of 64 travelled to the West, spreading His father's message of love and unity. He returned to Haifa just before World War One and the British Government knighted Him for His services to the poor. Abdul Baha passed away on 28 November 1921 and is buried in one of the rooms of the shrine of the Bab.

Abdul Baha wrote a Will and Testament in which He passed the guardianship of the faith and interpreter of the Baha'i scriptures to his grandson, Shoghi Effendi.
Shoghi Effendi dedicated his life to putting Baha'u'llah's plans into reality. He established the structures of the administration within the faith; he designed and constructed the gardens and shrines at the world centre of the Baha'i Faith in Israel. He also translated many of the holy writings into English, plus he wrote books himself, giving us a deeper understanding of the Faith. He devoted himself to helping people understand and develop the faith around the world. After his passing in 1957 in London, the 'Hands of the Cause',

previously appointed by Shoghi Effendi, took care of the faith. In 1963, following Baha'u'llah's original guidance, the Universal House of Justice was elected into being. Now it is the Universal House of Justice which is the centre of the administrative order of the faith.

This is a very brief history indeed, but I hope to have given you a small insight into where my quotes for this book have originated from.

I have used quotes from the Bab, Baha'u'llah, and Abdul Baha, which are authoritative writings from the Baha'i Faith. These are written in italics.

I have used quotes from Doctor John E Esslemont, who spent two and a half months with Abdul Baha whilst writing his book, 'Baha'u'llah and the New Era'. This book, although excellent, does not constitute authoritative writings of the faith.

There are references from a few other authors, again not authoritative writings from the Baha'i Faith.

In my book if a quote is not referenced it is not from the writings of the faith. It is my opinion and must not be taken as Baha'i teachings.

The Baha'i faith has many writings about the importance of medical science and consulting a physician. This book is looking at the spiritual side of healing and ways in which we can help ourselves.

'Spiritual health is conducive to physical health......
When the material world and the divine world are well correlated,
When the hearts become heavenly and the aspirations pure,
Perfect connections shall take place....
Physical and spiritual diseases will then receive absolute healing.' [79]

Baha'u'llah

If you wish to explore your healing abilities, please contact me for further information or workshops. I run workshops on all the self-help skills discussed in this book, for groups or individuals.

At the time of writing this book I live in Warwickshire, England. If you wish to contact me, my website is www.naturalhealingshop.co.uk

With respect to healing workshops, I will help you discover your own abilities and how to use them. Or you may have individual healing sessions to help you with physical, mental, emotional, or spiritual aspects of your life.

References

1. Epistle to the Son of the Wolf   US Bahá'í Publishing Trust, 1988 pocket-size edition   p14

2. Tablets of Bahá'u'lláh Revealed After the Kitáb-i-Aqdas
Author: Bahá'u'lláh Source: US Bahá'í Publishing Trust, 1988 pocket-size edition P157

3. Abdu'l-Baha Paris Talks p174

4. From a letter written on behalf of Shoghi Effendi to an individual believer, January 25, 1943: Spiritual Foundations: Prayer, Meditation, and the Devotional Attitude. (Compilations, Lights of Guidance, p. 455)

5. Bahá'u'lláh and the New Era   An Introduction to the Bahá'í Faith
By Dr. J.E. Esslemont Bahá'í Publishing Trust, Wilmette, Illinois   1980

6. Shoghi Effendi, Lights of Guidance, P. 456

7. Tablets of Abdul-Baha vii "Tablets of Abdul-Baha Abbas" Translated by Edward G. Browne Bahá'í Publishing Committee, New York 1980

8. Bahá'u'lláh's Teachings on Spiritual Reality compiled by Paul Lample p99

9. Promulgation of Universal Peace 'Abdu'l-Bahá p239 Talks Delivered by 'Abdu'l-Bahá during His Visit to the United States and Canada in 1912 Compiled by Howard MacNutt.

10. Taken from Some Answered Questions -Abdu'l-Baha   US Bahá'í Publishing Trust, 1990   PP143, 208.

11. Bahá'u'lláh's Teachings on Spiritual Reality compiled by Paul Lample p2

12. Adib Taherzadeh, The Covenant of Baha'u'llah p20 (Bahá'í Publishing Trust, London, 1972)

13. Adib Taherzadeh, The Covenant of Baha'u'llah p20 (Bahá'í Publishing Trust, London, 1972)

14. The Dalai Lama book of daily meditations P31 Compiled and edited by Renuka Singh Published by Rider

15. From a letter written on behalf of Shoghi Effendi, dated October 25, 1942, to an individual believer, p. 2 (Compilations, Lights of Guidance, p. 515)

16. Dr. J.E. Esslemont 'Bahá'u'lláh and the New Era' US Bahá'í Publishing Trust, 1980 edition Page 193

17. From a letter written on behalf of Shoghi Effendi, dated May 6, 1952, to an individual believer, p. 4 (Compilations, Lights of Guidance, p. 515)

18. Foundations Of World Unity By 'Abdu'l-Bahá   Bahá'í Publishing Trust, Wilmette, Illinois 1945

19. Baha'i World Faith (Abdu'l-Bahá's section only) Bahá'í Publishing Trust, Wilmette, Illinois 1976

20. Bahá'u'lláh and the New Era Author: Dr. J. E. Esslemont Source: US Bahá'í Publishing Trust, 1980 edition P192

21. Paris Talks. Talks delivered by 'Abdu'l-Bahá during His visits to Paris in 1911 & 1913

22. Promulgation of Universal Peace. Talks Delivered by 'Abdu'l-Bahá p246
during his visit to the United States and Canada in 1912. Compiled by Howard MacNutt

23. "Bahá'í World Faith" (Abdu'l-Bahá's section only) p267 Bahá'í Publishing Trust, Wilmette, Illinois 1976

24. From a letter written on behalf of Shoghi Effendi to an individual believer, August 22, 1957: From a compilation by the Research Department on behalf of the Universal House of Justice on 'Teaching', p. 18   (Compilations, Lights of Guidance, p. 461)

25. Principles of Bahá'í Administration P90   Bahá'í Publishing Trust, London 1950

26. Some Answered Questions By 'Abdu'l-Bahá p256 Collected and Translated by Laura Clifford Barney   Bahá'í Publishing Trust, Wilmette, Illinois 1981

27. The Compilation of Compilations Prepared by the Universal House of Justice 1963-1990, Volume I" p475 1991 Bahá'í Publications Australia ISBN 0 90991 55 3

28. Tablets of Abdul-Baha Abbas Vol. III   Translated by Edward G. Browne p654 Bahá'í Publishing Committee, New York 1980

29. Bahá'u'lláh and the New Era   Author: Dr. J. E. Esslemont Source: US Bahá'í Publishing Trust, 1980 edition P112

30. Baha'u'llah, Tablet to a Physician. Bahá'u'lláh and the New Era
Author: Dr. J. E. Esslemont Source: US Bahá'í Publishing Trust, 1980 edition P. 112

31. Selections From The Writings Of Abdu'l-Baha   p162   1978

32. Bahá'u'lláh and the New Era   Author: Dr. J. E. Esslemont Source: US Bahá'í Publishing Trust, 1980 edition P112

33. Some Answered Questions by 'Abdu'l-Bahá p45   Collected and Translated by Laura Clifford Barney Bahá'í Publishing Trust, Wilmette, Illinois   1981

34. Bahá'u'lláh and the New Era Author: Dr. J. E. Esslemont Source: US Bahá'í Publishing Trust, 1980 edition P112

35. Selections From The Writings Of Abdu'l Baha   p162   1978

36. From a letter written on behalf of Shoghi Effendi (Compilations, Baha'i Prayers, p. 208) Baha'i Prayers   A Selection of Prayers Revealed by Bahá'u'lláh, The Báb, and 'Abdu'l-Bahá 1991

37. The Chosen Highway by Lady Blomfield (Sitarih Khanum) p192   Bahá'í Publishing Trust, Wilmette, Illinois U.S.A.   The Bahá'í Publishing Trust, London 1956

38. Dr. J.E. Esslemont 'Bahá'u'lláh and the New Era' US Bahá'í Publishing Trust, 1980 edition *Page 194*

39. Dr. J.E. Esslemont 'Bahá'u'lláh and the New Era' US Bahá'í Publishing Trust, 1980 edition *Page 194*

40. Dr. J.E. Esslemont 'Bahá'u'lláh and the New Era' US Bahá'í Publishing Trust, 1980 edition *Page 194*

41. Abdu'l-Baha   Baha'i World Volumes, Volume 1, P12.   Baha'i Publishing Trust, Wilmette. Illinois.

42. The Bab, Selections from the Writings of the Bab, p. 122
Bahá'í World Centre 1976   ISBN 0-85398-066-7

43. Abdu'l-Baha (Marzieh Gail, Summon Up Remembrance, p. 254) George Ronald Oxford 1987

44. Adib Taherzadeh, The Revelation of Baha'u'llah v 4, p. 217   1987

45. From a letter dated 28 April 1936 written on behalf of Shoghi Effendi to an individual believer (Compilations, The Compilation of Compilations vol II, p. 7) 1991

46. Tablets Of Baha'u'llah revealed after The Kitab-I-Aqdas   (Baha'u'llah, Tablets of Baha'u'llah) P156

47. The Compilation of Compilations vol. I, p. 171   Universal House of Justice 1963-1990, Volume I ISBN 0 90991 55 3

48. The Bab, Selections from the Writings of the Bab, p. 18   Universal House of Justice 1976

49. (From letter written on behalf of Shoghi Effendi to an individual believer, February 26, 1933: Bahá'í News, No. 80, p. 5 January 1934 (Compilations, Lights of Guidance, p. 474) Lights of Guidance: A Bahá'í Reference File" Compiled by Helen Bassett Hornby, New Delhi 1994 Edition

50. Abdul Baha - Divine Philosophy p135   At the suggestion of Abdul Baha these notes on Divine Philosophy, together with a short introductory history, have been compiled and published by Isabel Fraser Chamberlain

51. Abdul Baha - Divine Philosophy p134   At the suggestion of Abdul Baha these notes on Divine Philosophy, together with a short introductory history, have been compiled and published by Isabel Fraser Chamberlain

52. Abdul Baha - Divine Philosophy p136   At the suggestion of Abdul Baha these notes on Divine Philosophy, together with a short introductory history, have been compiled and published by Isabel Fraser Chamberlain

53. Baha'u'llah, Epistle to the Son of the Wolf, p. 147   Bahá'í Publishing Trust, Wilmette, Illinois 60091   1988 Edition   ISBN 0-87743-182-5

54. Baha'u'llah, Gleanings from the Writings of Baha'u'llah, p. 328
Bahá'í Publishing Trust, Wilmette, Illinois 60091   1983 Edition
ISBN 0-87743-187-5

55. Baha'u'llah, The Persian Hidden Words 40

56. Abdu'l-Baha, Baha'i World Faith - Abdu'l-Baha Section, p. 378
Bahá'í Publishing Trust, Wilmette, Illinois 1956 Edition, ISBN 0-87743-043-8

57. Tablets Of Baha'u'llah revealed after The Kitab-I-Aqdas   (Baha'u'llah, Tablets of Baha'u'llah, p155)

58. Abdu'l-Baha, Paris Talks, p. 178 Talks delivered by 'Abdu'l-Bahá during His visits to Paris in 1911 & 1913

59. "Epistle to the Son of the Wolf" by Bahá'u'lláh P.118   Bahá'í Publishing Trust, Wilmette, Illinois 1988

60. Abdu'l-Baha, Divine Philosophy, p.79 At the suggestion of Abdul Baha these notes on Divine Philosophy, together with a short introductory history, have been compiled and published by Isabel Fraser Chamberlain

61. Abdu'l-Baha, Some Answered Questions, p. 300   Collected and Translated by Laura Clifford Barney Bahá'í Publishing Trust, Wilmette, Illinois 1987 Edition ISBN 0-87743-190-6

62. Tablets Of Baha'u'llah revealed after The Kitab-I-Aqdas   (Baha'u'llah, Tablets of Baha'u'llah, p.156)

63. "Gleanings from the Writings of Bahá'u'lláh" p.250 Bahá'í Publishing Trust, Wilmette, Illinois 1983 Edition   ISBN 0-87743-187-5

64. Abdu'l-Baha, Abdu'l-Baha in London, p. 19

65. "Some Answered Questions" by 'Abdu'l-Bahá p300   Collected and Translated by Laura Clifford Barney Bahá'í Publishing Trust, Wilmette, Illinois   1987 Edition ISBN 0-87743-190-6

66. Abdu'l-Baha, Paris Talks, p. 179 Talks delivered by 'Abdu'l-Bahá during His visits to Paris in 1911 & 1913

67. Foundations of World Unity" by 'Abdu'l-Bahá p.89   Bahá'í Publishing Trust, Wilmette, Illinois   1968

68. The Hidden words of Baha'u'llah – from the Arabic (5)

69. Baha'u'llah, Prayers and Meditations by Baha'u'llah, p. 240   Bahá'í Publishing Trust, Wilmette, Illinois 1987 Edition   ISBN 0-87743-024-1

70. "Selections from the Writings of Abdu'l-Bahá" P.51
Bahá'í World Centre, Haifa 1978   1982 Imprint   ISBN 0-87743-190-6

71. "Bahá'í Prayers, A Selection of Prayers Revealed by Bahá'u'lláh, The Báb, and 'Abdu'l-Bahá" 1991 Edition Bahá'í Publishing Trust Wilmette, Illinois

72. Bahá'u'lláh, The Arabic Hidden Words 21

73. Promulgation of Universal Peace 'Abdu'l-Bahá p.8 Talks delivered by 'Abdu'l-Bahá During His Visit to The United States and Canada in 1912 Compiled by Howard MacNutt

74. Abdu'l-Baha, The Secret of Divine Civilization, p. 103

75. Paris Talks   'Abdu'l-Bahá P.176   Talks delivered by 'Abdu'l-Bahá during His visits to Paris in 1911 & 1913

76. Abdu'l-Baha, The Promulgation of Universal Peace, p. 185   Talks Delivered by 'Abdu'l-Bahá   During His Visit to The United States and Canada in 1912 Compiled by Howard MacNutt

77. Abdu'l-Baha, Foundations of World Unity, p. 63   Bahá'í Publishing Trust, Wilmette, Illinois   1968

78. The Hidden Words of Bahá'u'lláh   Author: Bahá'u'lláh Source: US Bahá'í Publishing Trust, 1985 reprint Page 3

79. Bahá'u'lláh quoted in Bahá'u'lláh and the New Era Author: Dr. J. E. Esslemont Source: US Bahá'í Publishing Trust, 1980 edition P114

CPSIA information can be obtained
at www.ICGtesting.com
Printed in the USA
LVOW10s1841100117

520463LV00015B/739/P